Editor
Eric Migliaccio

Managing Editor
Ina Massler Levin, M.A.

Editor-in-Chief
Sharon Coan, M.S. Ed.

Illustrator
Sue Fullam

Cover Artist
Janet Chadwick

Art Coordinator
Kevin Barnes

Art Director
CJae Froshay

Imaging
Rosa C. See

Product Manager
Phil Garcia

Publisher
Mary D. Smith, M.S. Ed.

Spelling

GRADE 3

Author

Debra J. Housel, M.S. Ed.

Teacher Created Resources, Inc.
6421 Industry Way
Westminster, CA 92683
www.teachercreated.com

ISBN 13: 978-0-7439-3773-3

©2003 Teacher Created Resources, Inc.
Reprinted, 2007
Made in U.S.A.

Table of Contents

Introduction

The old adage "practice makes perfect" can really hold true for your child's education. The more practice and exposure your child has with concepts being taught in school, the more success he or she is likely to find. For many parents, knowing how to help their child may be frustrating because the resources may not be readily available. As a parent, it is also difficult to know where to focus your efforts so that the extra practice your child receives at home supports what he or she is learning in school.

This book has been written to help parents and teachers reinforce basic skills with children. *Practice Makes Perfect: Spelling* covers basic spelling skills for third graders. The exercises in this book can be completed in any order. The practice included in this book will meet or reinforce educational standards and objectives similar to the ones required by your state and school district for third graders:

- The student will recognize the spelling patterns for short and long vowel sounds.

- The student will recognize the sounds and spelling patterns for paired vowels.

- The student will know hard and soft /c/ sounds and spellings.

- The student will know hard and soft /g/ sounds and spellings.

- The student will understand consonant digraphs and consonant pairs with silent letters.

- The student will spell common contractions correctly.

- The student will spell high-frequency words, the 1,000 words that make up 90% of all written material. The majority of the words in these spelling lessons are these high-frequency words.

How to Make the Most of This Book

Here are some ideas for making the most of this book:

- Set aside a specific place in your home to work on this book. Keep it neat and tidy, with the necessary materials on hand.

- Determine a specific time of day to work on these practice pages to establish consistency. Look for times in your day or week that are less hectic and more conducive to practicing skills.

- Keep all practice sessions with your child positive and constructive. If your child becomes frustrated or tense, do not force your child to perform. Set the book aside and try again another time.

- Review and praise the work your child has done.

- Allow the child to use whatever writing instrument he or she prefers. For example, colored pencils add variety and pleasure to drill work.

- Introduce the spelling words in the list. Discuss how the words are different and how they are alike. Read the "In Context" column together. Be sure that the students understand the meaning of each word. Stress how words that are spelled alike often rhyme.

- Assist the student in understanding directions and decoding sentences.

- Encourage the child to point out spelling words, past and present, in the books, newspapers, and magazines he or she reads.

Contractions

Contractions are the blending of two words by shortening the second.

- For *not*, replace the "o" with an apostrophe. (n't)
- For *have*, replace the "ha" with an apostrophe ('ve)
- For *are*, replace the "a" with an apostrophe. ('re)
- For *will*, replace the "wi" with an apostrophe. ('ll)

Here are some common contractions used in English:

Contractions	Words	In Context
can't	can + not	He **can't** fit in that outfit.
wasn't	was + not	She **wasn't** in the room.
isn't	is + not	The money **isn't** in there.
won't	will + not	You **won't** tell anyone, will you?
don't	do + not	I **don't** understand.
didn't	did + not	They **didn't** shut the door.
doesn't	does + not	This TV **doesn't** work right.
could've	could + have	I'm sure that he **could've** helped me.
would've	would + have	If I knew he was coming, I **would've** waited.
you're	you + are	I know the place where **you're** staying.
we're	we + are	While **we're** inside, please keep quiet.
they're	they + are	We think **they're** seated over there.
I'll	I + will	Next week **I'll** go to the fair.
you'll	you + will	Tomorrow **you'll** go to the doctor.
we'll	we + will	This year **we'll** learn more math facts.

Using the information above, list the contractions in the correct column of the chart.

Are	*Have*	*Will*	*Not*

Contractions *(cont.)*

Word Equations

Copy the contractions from your lesson. Fill in the chart.

Contraction	Shorter Form of	Contraction
ex. shouldn't	should not	shouldn't
1.		
2.		
3.		
4.		
5.		
6.		
7.		
8.		
9.		
10.		
11.		
12.		
13.		
14.		
15.		

16. Write a different contraction using "not": _____

17. Write a different contraction using "will": _____

18. Write a different contraction using "have": _____

Spelling Pattern "igh"

The letters "igh" stand for long "i." The "g" and the "h" are always silent. This is just one of those odd spelling patterns that you have to get used to.

Words	In Context
tight	These pants are too **tight** on me.
light	Please turn off that **light**.
might	He **might** still be in the parking lot.
night	Last **night** my dog was lost.
fight	Let's not **fight** about this.
flight	What time is your **flight**?
right	Do you use your **right** hand to write?
bright	It was a **bright**, sunny day.
frighten	I didn't mean to **frighten** you.
sigh	Alex gave a **sigh**.
sight	There is no land in **sight**.
slightly	Move it **slightly** to the left.
knight	The **knight** rode a horse.
high	That shelf is too **high** for me to reach.
highway	The car broke down on the **highway**.

Choose the best word from the list to complete each sentence. Write it on the line. Use each word just once. Skip those you can't figure out. Go back once you've done the others.

1. If you _____ the baby, he may cry.

2. Lee felt like giving up. She heaved a big _____.

3. The truck turned onto the _____.

4. If you ask her, she _____ bring the cake.

5. Please turn the table _____ to the left.

6. Jim and Don got in trouble for starting a _____.

7. In the middle of the _____ I woke up.

8. The _____ light hurt my eyes.

9. It may not fit. It'll be a _____ squeeze.

10. A _____ often wore a metal suit during battle.

11. Our long _____ landed at 2 a.m.

12. Did you have the _____ answer for number six?

13. In the dim _____ of the candle, I couldn't read the book.

14. She reached down from _____ above me.

15. The Statue of Liberty is a beautiful _____.

Spelling Pattern: "igh" *(cont.)*

Using a Dictionary

> Guide words are in dark print at the top of each dictionary page. You look at them to see if the word you want falls *between* them.

Write each word from your lesson. Look up each one in a dictionary. What are the two guide words at the top of the page? Write the guide words.

Spelling Word	Left-side Guide Word	Right-side Guide Word
ex. delight	degrade	delirium
1.		
2.		
3.		
4.		
5.		
6.		
7.		
8.		
9.		
10.		
11.		
12.		
13.		
14.		
15.		

Spelling Pattern: "ing"

The spelling pattern "ing" is found in a great many words.

Words	In Context
king	The **king** sat on his throne.
sing	She likes to **sing**.
ring	The man wore a silver **ring**.
bring	Please **bring** me some tea.
spring	In the **spring** the flowers will bloom again.
wing	That bird hurt its **wing**.
thing	Do you know what that **thing** is used for?
being	Bob is **being** very helpful.
nothing	There's **nothing** in the box.
anything	Can I do **anything** to help you?
everything	Did you find **everything** you need?
something	Is **something** the matter?
morning	We get on the bus each **morning** at 8:20 A.M.
during	It happened **during** the night.
building	We went into the tall **building**.

Is the **dark word** spelled incorrectly in the sentences below? If it is right, circle **OK**. If it is not correct, write it correctly on the line provided.

1. As it turned, the plane's **wing** dipped.   OK _____

2. I said **nohing**.   OK _____

3. Where is that **thing** I gave you yesterday?   OK _____

4. Did the tree fall **dering** the storm?   OK _____

5. Is **everthing** all right?   OK _____

6. The best season of all is **spring**.   OK _____

7. Did I say **something** wrong?   OK _____

8. He gave her a beautiful **ring**.   OK _____

9. I can't find **enything** to wear!   OK _____

10. Tomorrow **moning** we'll go to the store.   OK _____

11. Please **bring** me a dozen eggs.   OK _____

12. The bird in the tree began to **sing**.   OK _____

13. We went up to the 13th story of the **bilding**.   OK _____

14. Why is he **bing** so rude?   OK _____

15. He is playing the role of the **king**.   OK _____

Spelling Pattern: "ing" *(cont.)*

Word Chain

Write each spelling word from the lesson inside a link of this chain:

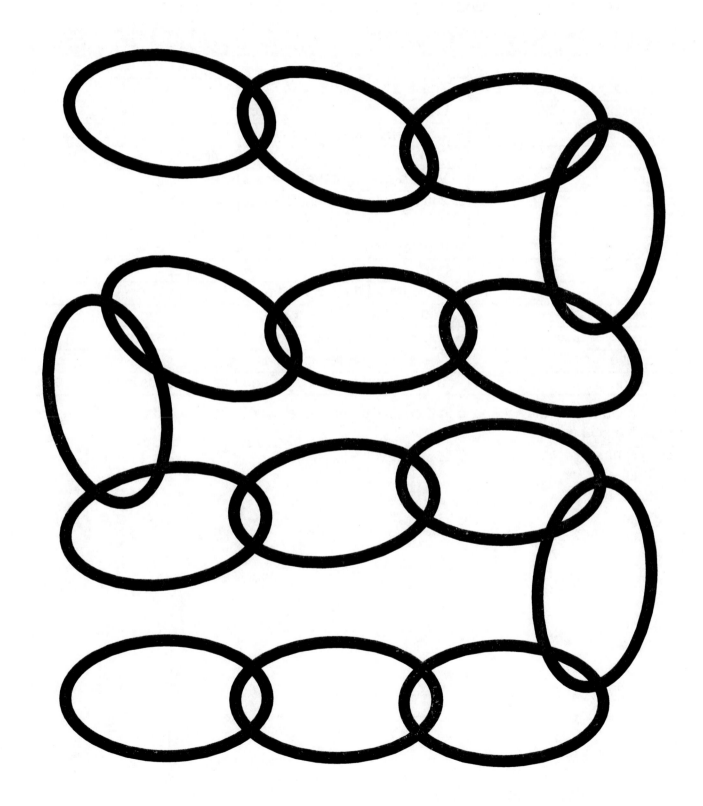

Consonant Pairs: "ph" & "tw"

Here are a few rules to remember:

- The digraph "ph" makes the /f/ sound.
- The letters "tw" are a blend of the sounds each letter makes by itself.

Words	In Context
phone	The **phone** rang.
photo	That's a beautiful **photo**.
physical	We go to **physical** education class on Wednesdays.
elephant	The **elephant** swung its long trunk.
alphabet	Can your little sister say the **alphabet**?
graph	Make a **graph** of the different types of coins.
paragraph	You need to add another **paragraph**.
twin	This is my **twin** brother.
twig	A **twig** snapped under her feet.
twice	I've called you **twice**.
twirl	Look at that dancer **twirl** around.
twist	Can you **twist** off the cap?
tweezers	You can pull out the sliver with these **tweezers**.
twelve	There are **twelve** months in one year.
twilight	The time between sunset and total darkness is **twilight**.

Write a word from the list above that ends with the same sound as the word given. Each word is used just once.

ex. sprinkle _____twinkle_____

1. girl _____

2. laugh _____

3. fist _____

4. nice _____

5. pickle _____

6. autograph _____

7. shelve* _____

8. infant _____

9. bone _____

10. upset _____

11. midnight _____

12. fig _____

13. shin _____

14. freezers _____

15. auto _____

*Used as a verb: "Please shelve the books correctly."

Consonant Pairs: "ph" & "tw" (cont.)

Word Scramble

Unscramble the spelling words. Put the letters on the lines that match the numbers to get the riddle's answer.

example: kmcu   m̲ u̲ c̲ k̲
            1 2   3

1. nwti   ___ ___ ___ ___
          4

2. hnoep ___ ___ ___ ___ ___
                    5

3. nlehatpe ___ ___ ___ ___ ___ ___ ___ ___
             6   7

4. triwl ___ ___ ___ ___ ___
                8

5. ghpra ___ ___ ___ ___
              9

6. tciew ___ ___ ___ ___ ___

7. gitw   ___ ___ ___ ___
                  10

8. toohp ___ ___ ___ ___ ___
              11   12

9. ttswi ___ ___ ___ ___ ___
                  13

10. etwvle ___ ___ ___ ___ ___ ___

11. clayship ___ ___ ___ ___ ___ ___ ___ ___
              14

12. steezwer ___ ___ ___ ___ ___ ___ ___ ___

13. apraghpra ___ ___ ___ ___ ___ ___ ___ ___ ___

14. tighliwt ___ ___ ___ ___ ___ ___ ___ ___

15. phaalteb ___ ___ ___ ___ ___ ___ ___ ___

What did one penny say to the other?

___ ___ m̲ ___ ___ ___ ___ ___ ___ ___ ___ ___ ___ ___
8 4   1 7 3 6 13   13 6 5 13 6   4 12

___ ___ ___ ___ ___ ___ ___ ___ ___ ___ ___ ___ ___!
14 2 4   2 13   4 12 10 6 4 11 6 9

Consonant Pairs: "wr" & "kn"

These consonant pairs have a silent letter:

- The letters "wr" make the /r/ sound (the "w" is silent).
- The letters "kn" make the /n/ sound (the "k" is silent).

Words	In Context
wrap	Please **wrap** these gifts.
wreck	The icy roads caused a car **wreck**.
wrong	It's **wrong** to hit others.
wrote	I **wrote** a letter to my brother.
writer	Who is the **writer** of that book?
wreath	Let's hang a pretty **wreath** on our door.
wriggle	The puppy woke up and started to **wriggle**.
wrinkle	If you iron the skirt, it will get rid of that **wrinkle**.
knit	Does your mom know how to **knit**?
knot	Tie the **knot** so that it won't come loose.
knife	Be careful with that **knife**!
knock	I will **knock** on the door.
knuckles	His **knuckles** are sore.
known	How long have you **known** about this problem?
knowledge	It's always good to get more **knowledge**.

Circle the word that's spelled correctly. Copy it on the line.

1. nown   knowne   known   _____
2. reath   wreath   wreth   _____
3. knife   nife   knief   _____
4. wrap   rwap   wrop   _____
5. knowedge   nowledge   knowledge   _____
6. writter   writer   riter   _____
7. knuckles   knuckels   nuckels   _____
8. wrek   reck   wreck   _____
9. nit   knitt   knit   _____
10. knock   nock   knok   _____
11. rong   wrong   wreng   _____
12. wrigle   wriggel   wriggle   _____
13. knott   knot   nott   _____
14. wrout   roet   wrote   _____
15. wrinkle   wrinkel   rinkle   _____

Consonant Pairs: "wr" & "kn" *(cont.)*

Phone Code

Telephones have numbers and letters on their keys. Copy each spelling word. Then write the word again using its numbers.

	Spelling Word	Phone Code for Word
ex.	wrench	973624
1.		
2.		
3.		
4.		
5.		
6.		
7.		
8.		
9.		
10.		
11.		
12.		
13.		
14.		
15		

Hard "C" and Hard "G"

Usually when the letters "c" and "g" are followed by the vowels "a," "o," or "u," the initial consonant is hard. A hard "c" sounds like the letter "k." A hard "g" sounds like the "g" in "gate."

Words	In Context
carry	Can you **carry** that much?
careful	Please be **careful** walking on the ice.
could	I'd like to know if you **could** attend my party.
come	If you **come**, will you bring a game?
color	I like the **color** pink the best.
cute	Your kitten is just so **cute**!
curve	Slow down for that sharp **curve**.
gave	He **gave** her a book.
garden	She planted flowers in her **garden**.
gather	They like to **gather** leaves each fall.
guard	The **guard** wouldn't let them in the door.
guess	I **guess** that you're upset with me.
going	Where are we **going** on vacation?
gone	Ruth has **gone** to the store.
government	We choose the people who run our **government**.

Copy the words. Number them in order from A–Z. You may need to look as far as the third letter. Then write the words in A–Z order.

Word	Number	A–Z Order
1.		
2.		
3.		
4.		
5.		
6.		
7.		
8.		
9.		
10.		
11.		
12.		
13.		
14.		
15.		

Hard "C" and Hard "G" *(cont.)*

Crossword Puzzle

Choose the spelling word that would best complete each clue below.

Across

1. The _____ stood watch alone.
3. Is green your favorite _____?
6. The _____ runs the country.
7. Be _____ not to slip on the ice.
8. By then we had already _____ down the stairs.
10. Sam _____ her a doll.
11. The flowers in your _____ are beautiful.

Down

1. Please _____ the papers together.
2. Please _____ to visit me soon.
3. That teddy bear is very _____.
4. He _____ not go to see the movie.
5. The boy threw a _____ ball.
8. Where are you _____ on vacation?
9. Can you _____ all those bags?
10. Can you _____ what number I'm thinking of?

Soft "C" and Soft "G"

Usually when the letters "c" and "g" are followed by the letters "e" or "i," the initial consonant is soft. A soft "c" sounds like the letter "s." A soft "g" sounds like the letter "j."

Words	In Context
certain	Are you **certain** she's gone?
cereal	They eat many kinds of **cereal**.
cents	Do you have 50 **cents**?
center	Let's sit in the **center** of the room.
celebrate	Did you **celebrate** on your birthday?
circle	Can you draw a perfect **circle**?
circus	He wants to see the **circus** this weekend.
cider	She likes to drink apple **cider**.
citizen	Being a U.S. **citizen** gives you rights.
germs	How do **germs** pass from one person to another?
generous	The woman was **generous** with her money.
gentle	Todd was very **gentle** with the frog.
general	As a **general** rule, don't talk with food in your mouth.
giant	The **giant** bent down to pick up the man.
gigantic	There's a **gigantic** sale at the mall today.

Is the **dark word** spelled wrong in the sentences below? If it is right, circle **OK**. If it is not correct, write it correctly on the line provided.

1. To an ant, a person must look like a **giant**.　　OK　_____

2. Wash your hands to stop **germs** from spreading.　　OK　_____

3. In that photo, Jerry is in the **center**.　　OK　_____

4. Would you like a glass of warm apple **sider**?　　OK　_____

5. The children sat in a big **circle**.　　OK　_____

6. He ate a **gigantic** dinner.　　OK　_____

7. The **general** liked to go for a daily walk.　　OK　_____

8. Is that the kind of **ceral** that you like best?　　OK　_____

9. He is **certain** that he locked the door.　　OK　_____

10. People **celbrate** Christmas on December 25.　　OK　_____

11. She is a **citizen** of Mexico.　　OK　_____

12. Can you lend me ten **cents**?　　OK　_____

13. They gave a **genrous** gift of money.　　OK　_____

14. The pig liked how **gental** the girl was.　　OK　_____

15. Those horses are part of the **cirkus**.　　OK　_____

Soft "C" and Soft "G" *(cont.)*

Paint Can Word Sort

In the word bank are words from Lessons 6 and 7. Think about the rules for hard and soft letters. Sort the words based on their beginning sounds. Write the words on the correct can.

Word Bank				
germ	carry	government	certain	come
cereal	careful	guess	gone	circus
going	general	cents	circle	gigantic
could	center	gave	guard	celebrate
gather	color	cider	curve	garden
gentle	cute	giant	generous	citizen

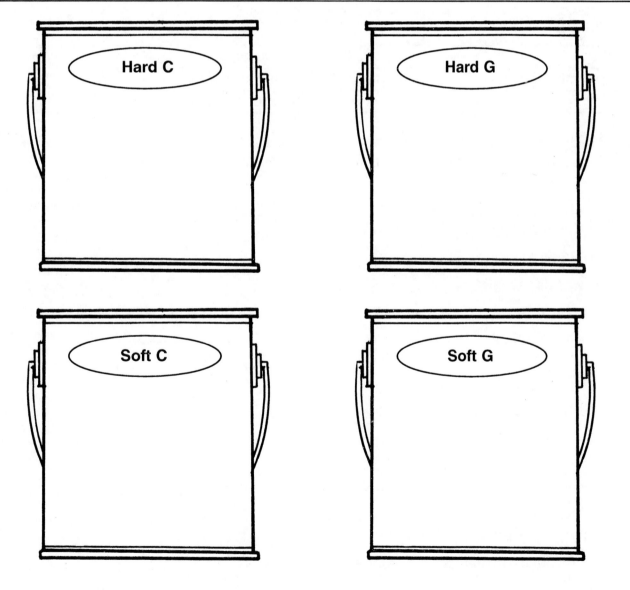

Hard C

Hard G

Soft C

Soft G

The Letter "a" at the End of a Word

When a word ends with the letter "a," the "a" sounds like "uh" (as in "uh huh").

Words	In Context
pizza	The food I like best is **pizza**.
comma	A period is different from a **comma**.
idea	We like your **idea** very much.
area	Put your books down in this **area**.
banana	Would you like a **banana**?
extra	She gave us three extra cookies.
china	He broke a piece of **china**.
camera	She took a picture with her **camera**.
lava	The hot **lava** flowed down the hill.
Canada	**Canada** is north of the U.S.A.
America	Do you live in **America**?
Africa	Many parts of **Africa** are hot and dry.
Asia	**Asia** is the largest continent.
Australia	**Australia** is the smallest continent.
Antarctica	**Antarctica** is the coldest continent.

Choose the best word from the list above to complete each sentence. Write it on the line. Use each word once. Skip those you can't figure out and go back to them once you've done the others.

1. The _____ came from the volcano.

2. She lives in the U.S.A., which is in North _____.

3. The fruit I like best is _____.

4. It was Jane's _____ to visit the zoo.

5. We have two _____ pieces of cake. Would you like one?

6. Soon the stage _____ was filled with smoke.

7. This is the best _____ I've ever eaten!

8. The biggest continent is _____.

9 You need to put a _____ after that word.

10. The world's coldest continent is _____.

11. The Sahara Desert is in _____.

12. I want to get some pictures. Did you remember to bring the _____?

13. He broke a piece of his mom's _____.

14. The world's littlest continent is _____.

15. One country that shares a border with the U.S.A. is _____.

The Letter "a" at the End of a Word *(cont.)*

Venn Diagram

Write the words with more consonants than vowels in the circle labeled "More Consonants."
Write the words with more vowels than consonants in the circle labeled "More Vowels."
In the middle, write the words that have the same number of consonants and vowels.

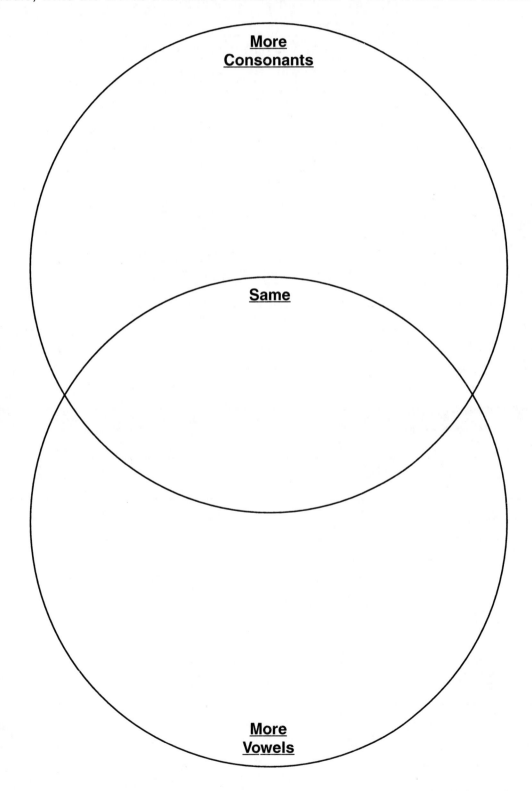

**More
Consonants**

Same

**More
Vowels**

"W" Affects "O"

The letter "w" affects any vowel that stands in front of it. In these words the "w" make the "o" say long /o/.

Words	In Context
row	Harry would like to sit in the back **row**.
grow	Moss will only **grow** in damp places.
low	The sun was already **low** in the sky.
blow	A strong wind began to **blow**.
flow	Water will always **flow** downhill.
slow	It's too **slow** to do it that way.
show	They can **show** you a better way.
snow	I'm sure that it will **snow** in December.
know	Do you **know** what time it is?
below	He reached **below** his seat and pulled out a box.
window	She opened the **window**.
narrow	I didn't know if I could fit through such a **narrow** opening.
shadow	We saw his **shadow** on the wall.
follow	Please **follow** me.
owner	Are you the **owner** of this house?

Copy the spelling words. If you can add "ed" to make a real word, write it in the second column. If you can add "s" to make a real word, write it in the third column. Some words can have both "ed" and "s" added to them. Others cannot have either "ed" or "s" added.

Spelling Word	Does adding "ed" make a real word?	Does adding "s" make a real word?
ex. arrow	NO	arrows
1.		
2.		
3.		
4.		
5.		
6.		
7.		
8.		
9.		
10.		
11.		
12.		
13.		
14.		
15.		

"W" Affects "O" *(cont.)*

Word Scramble

Unscramble the spelling words. Put each letter on the line that matches its number. You will form the answer to the riddle.

ex. tdcahte   c(19)   h(4)   a   t(3)   t(13)   e   d

1. lswo   ___(12) ___ ___ ___
2. fowl*   ___ ___ ___(15) ___
3. onwk   ___(20) ___ ___
4. sonw   ___(16) ___(1) ___ ___
5. wwdnio   ___ ___(5) ___ ___(22) ___ ___
6. blowe   ___ ___(21) ___ ___
7. wol   ___ ___(18) ___
8. bowl*   ___ ___ ___(10)
9. wrog   ___(7) ___ ___ ___
10. flowol   ___ ___ ___ ___(2) ___ ___
11. dahsow   ___ ___(8) ___(11) ___ ___ ___
12. wro   ___ ___(14) ___
13. wosh   ___ ___(17) ___ ___
14. nerow   ___ ___ ___ ___(9) ___
15. rowarn   ___(6) ___ ___ ___ ___ ___

* Yes, it's already a word, but please change the letters to form a spelling word from this lesson.

Question: What did Ben Franklin say when he discovered electricity?

Answer: ___ ___ ___ ___ ___ ___ ___! ___ ___ ___ ___ ___
   1   2   3   4   5   6   7   8   9   10   11   12

___ ___ ___ ___ ___ ___ ___ ___ ___ ___ .
13   14   15   16   17   18   19   20   21   22

"W" Affects "E"

The letter "w" affects any vowel that stands in front of it. Together they make a new sound. When you see "ew," it makes the long /u/ sound!

Words	In Context
new	He got a **new** jacket.
few	Only a **few** people know about this.
dew	The morning **dew** made the grass wet.
drew	She **drew** a map for me to use.
grew	They **grew** up in this town.
stew	Your **stew** smells really good.
chew	Be sure to **chew** your food before you swallow.
flew	The birds **flew** south for the winter.
blew	A cool breeze **blew** in from the lake.
knew	She **knew** how to read in first grade.
threw	Jim **threw** the ball to Ted.
crew	The ship's **crew** worked hard.
view	There's a good **view** of the mountain from this window.
review	You need to **review** your math facts.
preview	Before the movie, we saw a **preview**.

Circle the word that's spelled correctly. Copy it on the line.

1. grew   greu   grue   _____
2. prevew   preview   previw   _____
3. cheu   chewe   chew   _____
4. flue   flew   fleiw   _____
5. new   neu   newe   _____
6. vew   view   viwe   _____
7. few   fow   fewe   _____
8. thru   threwe   threw   _____
9. stue   stew   steiw   _____
10. knew   knewe   kneuw   _____
11. dru   dreiw   drew   _____
12. crue   crew   creew   _____
13. dew   du   deu   _____
14. blew   blewe   bliew   _____
15. rview   revew   review   _____

"W" Affects "E" *(cont.)*

Using a Dictionary

Write each word. Look up each one in a dictionary. What are the two guide words at the top of the page? Write the guide words.

Spelling Word	Left-side Guide Word	Right-side Guide Word
ex. screw	screech	scurvy
1.		
2.		
3.		
4.		
5.		
6.		
7.		
8.		
9.		
10.		
11.		
12.		
13.		
14.		
15.		

"W" Affects "O" Another Way

The letter "w" affects any vowel that stands in front of it. Together they make a new sound. When you see "ow," it usually says the vowel sound of "ou" as in "Ouch!"

Words	In Context
how	Do you know **how** to get there?
now	Must we leave right **now**?
cows	The **cows** ate grass.
down	She went **down** the ladder.
town	We live in a small **town**.
brown	He likes to wear **brown** pants.
crown	The queen lost her **crown**.
crowd	The **crowd** sang along with the singer.
allow	Did your dad **allow** you to go alone?
however	I grabbed for the keys; **however**, I couldn't reach them.
towel	This **towel** is wet.
vowel	The letter "o" is a **vowel**.
power	The worker used a **power** shovel to dig the hole.
shower	I take a **shower** each morning.
flowers	We gave the **flowers** to our teacher.

Draw a line to match the words that rhyme.

ex. vow ———————— wow

1. now   towers

2. crowd   shower

3. towel   town

4. power   loud

5. down   how

6. flowers   crown

7. cows   vowel

8. brown   plows

Which two spelling words are not used in the matching activity?

9. _____   10. _____

"W" Affects "O" Another Way *(cont.)*

Howling Hounds

If the "ow" says "O," color the hound gray. If the "ow" sounds like "ouch," color the hound brown.

below   towel   power

town   shadow   window

snow   shower   however

allow   flower   known

owner   vowel   crowd

Vowel pairs: "ou"

When two vowels stand together, the first one usually says its name. But some vowel pairs make a whole new sound. The vowel pair "ou" makes the sound you hear in "ouch!"

Words	In Context
found	We **found** this dollar bill on the sidewalk.
pound	He began to **pound** on the door.
round	She sat at a **round** table.
around	Let's go **around** to the back of the shed.
ground	The **ground** was damp from the rain.
sound	They didn't hear a **sound**.
about	Can you be here **about** 1 P.M.?
house	They plan to sell their **house** this summer.
without	I won't go **without** you.
mountain	The **mountain** had a cap of snow.
cloud	There wasn't a single **cloud** in the sky.
hours	After three **hours**, he finally showed up.
amount	The **amount** of the bill is $48.76.
south	Birds fly **south** for the winter.
mouth	Ouch! I just bit the inside of my **mouth**.

In the first column, copy each word. Next, write the words again with the vowel pair in a different color. Then write the words once more, and circle the vowel pair.

Word	Vowel pair "ou" in different color	Circle the vowel pair
1.		
2.		
3.		
4.		
5.		
6.		
7.		
8.		
9.		
10.		
11.		
12.		
13.		
14.		
15.		

Vowel pairs: "ou" *(cont.)*

Crossword Puzzle

Choose the spelling word that would best complete each clue below.

Across

5. Is your new pool _____ or oval?
7. He wants to climb that _____.
8. We swam all the way _____ the tiny island.
9. He went to the game _____ his friend.
12. We must drive _____ to reach the river.
14. I just heard _____ your problem.
15. A mouse lives in that hole in the _____.

Down

1. The _____ of the waves led them toward the water.
2. Something is stuck in his _____.
3. The woman lost another _____.
4. I _____ a little lost kitten.
6. He lost a large _____ of money in the stock market.
10. We'll move into our new _____ tomorrow.
11. Suddenly a _____ blocked the sun.
13. How many _____ did it take you to finish the work?

Vowel Pairs: "oo"

When two vowels stand together, usually the first one says its name. But some vowel pairs make a whole new sound instead. The vowel pair "oo" usually makes the long /u/ sound:

Words	In Context
too	Those clothes are **too** loose on you.
food	My favorite **food** is potato chips.
school	Where do you go to **school**?
soon	Jay will arrive here **soon**.
room	We want to stay in the biggest **room**.
moon	The **moon** seems to change size, but it really does not.
root	The plant died when its main **root** was cut.
cool	Her cheeks felt **cool**.
tool	Please hand me that **tool**.
pool	They plan to put a **pool** in their backyard.
choose	Which kind did you **choose**?
smooth	Their floor was **smooth** and shiny.
shoot	The hunters will **shoot** at the geese.
balloon	The red **balloon** went floating over our heads.
afternoon	Will you come visit me this **afternoon**?

Copy the words. Number them in order from A–Z. Write the words in A–Z order.

	Word	Number	A–Z Order
1.			
2.			
3.			
4.			
5.			
6.			
7.			
8.			
9.			
10.			
11.			
12.			
13.			
14.			
15.			

Vowel Pairs: "oo" *(cont.)*

Venn Diagram

Write the words with more consonants than vowels in the circle labeled "More Consonants."
Write the words with more vowels than consonants in the circle labeled "More Vowels."
In the middle write the words that have the same number of consonants and vowels.

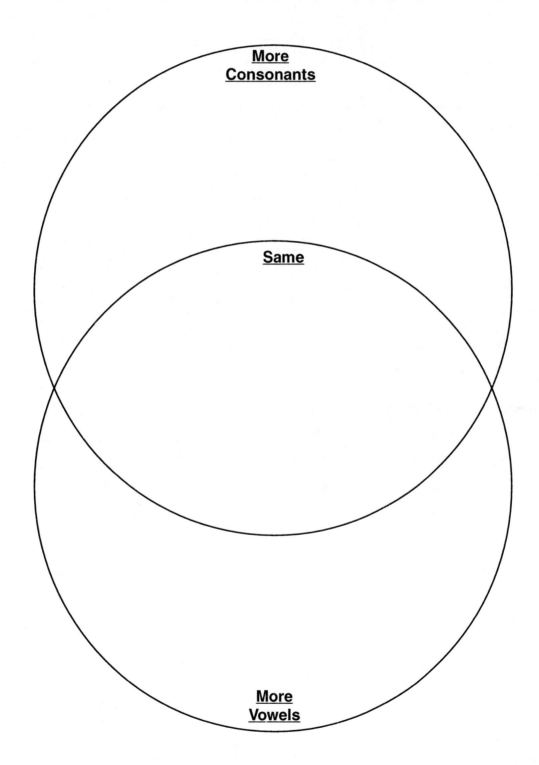

Vowel Pairs: "oi" & "oy"

When you see the vowel pairs "oi" or "oy," they form the sound you hear in "boy."

Words	In Context
oil	The recipe calls for one cup of **oil**.
soil	She spread the **soil** on the yard.
join	We want to **join** your club.
coin	Is that **coin** worth 25 cents?
point	I can **point** him out to you.
avoid	Let's **avoid** rush hour by leaving later.
voice	Her **voice** was very soft and sweet.
choice	He needs to make a **choice** between the blue and the orange.
noise	There's so much **noise** that I can't hear what you're saying!
toys	He plays with these **toys** every day.
enjoy	We **enjoy** seeing movies.
destroy	A lightning strike can **destroy** a tree.
loyal	He is a very **loyal** friend.
annoy	It will **annoy** us if you turn the music up.
employee	She needs to get a new **employee** for her store.

Circle the word that's spelled correctly. Copy it on the line.

1. goin   join   joyn   _____

2. employe   emploiee   employee   _____

3. oil   oile   oyl   _____

4. loial   loyal   loyall   _____

5. soyl   soile   soil   _____

6. toys   tois   toyes   _____

7. point   poynt   pointe   _____

8. coyn   coin   coine   _____

9. anoy   anoiy   annoy   _____

10. choise   choice   choyse   _____

11. avoid   avoide   avoyd   _____

12. noyse   noice   noise   _____

13. destroy   destoy   destroiy   _____

14. injoy   enjoy   enjoiy   _____

15. voyce   voise   voice   _____

Vowel Pairs: "oi" & "oy" *(cont.)*

Caterpillar

Write a spelling word on each segment of this caterpillar's body.

Vowel Pairs: "au" and "aw"

The letter "w" affects any vowel that stands in front of it. Together they make a new sound. When you see the vowel pairs "aw" or "au," they make the same sound as, "Aw, I don't want to go to bed!"

Words	In Context
saw	She **saw** the truck drive away.
draw	You can use a stick to **draw** in the sand.
paw	My dog cut its **paw**.
jaw	Dad rubbed his **jaw** as he thought.
raw	Never eat **raw** meat.
law	It is against the **law** to take things that aren't yours.
claws	The cat grabbed for the mouse with its **claws**.
flaw	Can you see the **flaw** in this fabric?
straw	Please bring me a **straw** for my milk.
drawing	Deb made a nice **drawing** of their home.
cause	What is the **cause** of that noise?
caught	Her sweater got **caught** in the door.
daughter	Their **daughter** is two years old.
autumn	Each **autumn** the leaves turn red, yellow, and orange.
automobile	The red **automobile** stopped at the light.

Is the **dark word** spelled wrong in the sentences below? If it is right, circle **OK**. If it is not correct, write it correctly on the line.

1. Next **autumn** I'll go to fourth grade.   OK _____
2. That's Mrs. Clark's **dauter**.   OK _____
3. The deer **saw** the wolf.   OK _____
4. The child made a **drawing** of her pets.   OK _____
5. What happened to **caws** this mess?   OK _____
6. It is against the **law** to take things that are not yours.   OK _____
7. He likes to drink his soup with a **straw**.   OK _____
8. Can you **draw** a map for me?   OK _____
9. The cabinet had a tiny **falw** in its door.   OK _____
10. A chipmunk got its **paw** stuck in our bird feeder.   OK _____
11. The black dog dug its **claus** into the dirt.   OK _____
12. Did you see the **automoble** accident yesterday?   OK _____
13. As she fell, she hit her **jaw**.   OK _____
14. Billy was **cought** with his hand in the cookie jar.   OK _____
15. Some people like to eat **raw** fish.   OK _____

Vowel Pairs: "au" and "aw" *(cont.)*

Phone Code

Telephones have numbers and letters on their keys. Write each word from your spelling lesson. Then write the word again using its numbers.

	Spelling Word	Phone Code for Word
ex.	lawyer	529937
1.		
2.		
3.		
4.		
5.		
6.		
7.		
8.		
9.		
10.		
11.		
12.		
13.		
14.		
15.		

16. Which three words have the same phone code?

_____ and _____ and _____

Vowel Pair: "oo"

When two vowels stand together, usually the first one says its name. But some vowel pairs make a whole new sound instead. The vowel pair "oo" usually makes the long /u/ sound. But sometimes it makes another sound, as in look. Here are some words with the less common "oo" sound:

Words	In Context
look	We will **look** inside the box.
took	Jed **took** a saw from the shed.
book	Will you please read me this **book**?
brook	The fish swam in the **brook**.
nook (small corner)	I sat in the **nook**, hidden from their view.
cook	My dad is a very good **cook**.
crook	The **crook** stole the money.
hook	Put your coat on the **hook** behind the door.
shook	I **shook** the rug to get rid of the dirt.
foot	Don't step on the baby's **foot**.
good	That's a **good** idea!
wood	We burn **wood** in our fireplace each winter.
hood	Put up your **hood** to keep your ears warm.
stood	They **stood** on the step, waiting for the door to open.
wool	She had on a **wool** scarf.

Choose the best word from the list above to complete each sentence. Write it on the line. Use each word once. Skip those you can't figure out and go back once you've done the others.

1. You can hang your jacket on this _____ behind the door.

2. She wore a heavy _____ cape.

3. Let's _____ in those store windows.

4. An old man _____ alone in the bean field.

5. I just stepped on a piece of glass and cut my _____.

6. Yesterday a _____ broke into the house.

7. Can you tell me the name of a good _____ to read?

8. The boy _____ off his wet clothes.

9. Her report showed that she had gotten _____ grades.

10. The baby fell into the _____, got all wet, and started to cry.

11. Please cut this _____ into smaller logs.

12. As the house _____, it made the dishes fall with a loud crash.

13. I want to learn how to _____ meals.

14. Sarah found the small chest hidden in a tiny _____ up in her attic.

15. Since his coat did not have a _____, his head got cold.

Vowel Pair: "oo" (cont.)

Bookshelves

These book titles use all of the words from Lessons 13 and 17.   Sort the titles based on their "oo" vowel sounds. Write each title on the spine of a book on the correct bookshelf.

Look Out!	The Magic Tool	A Wool Cloak	Full Moon	The Attic Nook
Good Times	He Took the Call	Come Home Soon	The Ugly Hook	The Blue Hood
Choose a Game	Smooth as Glass	Shoot the Stars	Hot Air Balloons	How to Cook
The Deep Pool	Hard as Wood	A Silly Book	A Tangled Root	The Dark Room
Play it Cool	Me Too!	Yummy Food	The Quiet Brook	Monster's Foot
One Scary Afternoon	The Secret Crook	It Stood on on the Hill	My Haunted School	The Day the World Shook

oo as in "cool"

oo as in "book"

Vowel Pair: "ea"

The vowel pair "ea" is tricky. It doesn't follow any set rules. Most of the time when you see "ea," it says long /e/. Yet in some words it says the short /e/ sound:

Words	In Context
bread	She baked three loaves of **bread**.
instead	I will use red ribbon **instead** of green.
ahead	We saw lights up **ahead**.
already	Have you **already** been inside the cave?
heavy	She picked up the **heavy** bag.
meant	He **meant** to say that he was sorry.
death	The queen ruled after the king's **death**.
breath	You could use a **breath** of fresh air.
weather	What's the **weather** like?
ocean	This **ocean** is miles deep in some places.
measure	Did you **measure** the hem for the dress?

Copy the spelling words. Make the changes to form a new word. Write the new word. Does the "ea" in the new word sound the same as the "ea" in the spelling word?

Spelling Word	Change	New Word	Same "ea" Sound?
ex. ready	replace "r" with "b"	beady	NO
1.	replace "b" with "t"		
2.	drop "in" add "y" to end		
3.	drop first "a"		
4.	drop "al"		
5.	replace "y" with "e"		
6.	drop "t"		
7.	replace "d" with "wr"		
8.	add "e" to end		
9.	replace "w" with "f"		
10.	replace "oc" with "cl"		
11.	replace "m" with "pl"		

Challenge: Can you think of a sentence for each spelling word that uses both the spelling word and its new word? *ex.* The cat with the <u>beady</u> eyes was <u>ready</u> to jump.

Vowel Pair: "ea" (cont.)

Bread Loaves Word Sort

In the word bank are all of the words from Lesson 17 and some other "ea" words. Think about the sounds made by the vowel pair "ea." Sort the words based on their vowel sounds. Write the words on the correct loaf of bread.

bear	scream	seats	already
heavy	ocean	weather	reading
treat	bread	steal	breath
measure	wear	ahead	speak
bead	meant	great	instead
death	repeat	leaf	break

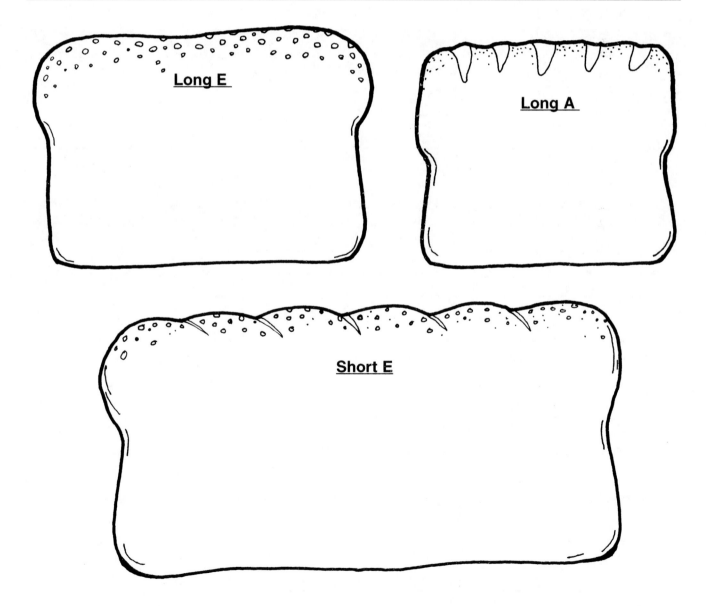

Long E

Long A

Short E

Vowel Pair: "ey"

The vowel pair "ey" is usually pronounced long /e/:

Words	In Context
key	The **key** didn't work in the door.
valley	A beautiful **valley** lay between the hills.
hockey	The ice **hockey** team played well.
alley	A narrow passage between two buildings is called an **alley**.
journey	His **journey** covered 700 miles.
honey	Bees make **honey**.
money	Alice likes getting **money** for her birthday.
turkey	The **turkey** tasted very good.
monkey	My favorite zoo animal is the **monkey**.
volleyball	Tim wants to make the **volleyball** team.

However, in a few words, "ey" is pronounced long /a/:

Words	In Context
hey	I heard someone shout **hey**!
they	**They** own a rabbit.
prey	The owl reached out to grab its **prey**.
obey	You should **obey** your parents.
disobey	Why did you **disobey** me?

Copy each spelling word. Write the vowel as an equation. Write the spelling word again.

Spelling Word	Equation	Spelling Word
ex. galley	$e + y = $ long e	galley
1.		
2.		
3.		
4.		
5.		
6.		
7.		
8.		
9.		
10.		
11.		
12.		
13.		
14.		
15.		

Vowel Pair: "ey" (cont.)

Using a Dictionary

Guide words are in dark print at the top of each dictionary page. You look at them to see if the word you want falls *between* them.

Write each word. Look up each one in a dictionary. What are the two guide words at the top of the page? Write the guide words.

Spelling Word	Left-side Guide Word	Right-side Guide Word
ex. kidney	ketchup	kill
1.		
2.		
3.		
4.		
5.		
6.		
7.		
8.		
9.		
10.		
11.		
12.		
13.		
14.		
15.		

Vowel Pairs: "io" & "eo"

The vowel pair "io" often says "I-uh."

Words	In Context
violet	You look beautiful in the color **violet**.
pioneer	He went West as a **pioneer** during the 1860s.
prior	Brush your teeth **prior** to going to bed. (*before*)
priority	Doing well in school should be your top **priority**.
violin	She is learning to play the **violin**.
violent	It is not wise to be **violent**.
Iowa	We live in the state of **Iowa**.

Sometimes "io" says "ee-oh." Other words that end in this sound are spelled "eo."

Words	In Context
radio	Please turn off the **radio**.
ratio	The **ratio** of 2 to 3 is written 2:3.
trio	A **trio** is a group of three.
patio	They had lunch on their **patio**.
studio	The rock star sang in a **studio**.
rodeo	The cowboy tried to stay on the horse during the **rodeo**.
video	I want to rent a **video** so we can watch it tonight.
stereo	The car's **stereo** speakers were broken.

Circle the word that's spelled correctly. Copy it on the line.

1. sterio   stereo   stero   _____
2. patio   pateo   paito   _____
3. vilet   violt   violet   _____
4. Iowa   iowa   ioa   _____
5. rodio   rodo   rodeo   _____
6. priorty   priority   prioty   _____
7. radeo   radio   radieo   _____
8. treo   treio   trio   _____
9. violin   violen   violine   _____
10. pioner   pionere   pioneer   _____
11. vidio   video   viodeo   _____
12. prier   priore   prior   _____
13. violent   vielent   vialent   _____
14. studeo   studio   stoodio   _____
15. rashio   rateo   ratio   _____

Vowel Pairs: "io" & "eo" *(cont.)*

Crossword Puzzle

Choose the spelling word that would best complete each clue below.

Across

1. What school were you in _____ to coming here?
4. That flower is a _____.
6. We live in the state of _____.
7. My top _____ is to learn math.
8. The girl stayed on the bull during the _____.
10. A _____ is a group of three people.
11. Those _____ speakers have great sound.

Down

2. The _____ of 1/2 is written 1:2.
3. He drew the bow across his _____.
4. If you do something _____, you may go to jail.
5. Dad grilled steaks out on the _____.
7. He was a _____ during the 1840s.
8. You listen to music on the _____.
9. I watched a rented _____ today.
11. The artist's _____ was upstairs.

Vowel Pair: "ie"

When you see the vowel pair "ie" in a one-syllable word, it says long /i/:

Words	In Context
pie	He really likes to eat cherry **pie**.
die	The chipmunk must find food or **die**.
tie	When did you learn to **tie** your shoes?
lie	It's best to tell the truth instead of telling a **lie**.

Most of the time the vowel pair "ie" says long /e/:

Words	In Context
piece	We shared the **piece** of cake.
field	The **field** was full of weeds.
believe	I **believe** that the show is going to be next week.
chief	The **chief** of the tribe danced around the fire.
series	We plan on watching that TV **series**.
movie	Did you enjoy the **movie**?
experience	What's the best **experience** you ever had?

However, right after the letter "c," the vowel pair's letters are changed to "ei."

Words	In Context
receive	What did you **receive** for your birthday?
receipt	When you buy something in a store, you get a **receipt**.
ceiling	The ketchup hit the **ceiling** and made a stain.
deceit (*dishonesty*)	Lying is a form of **deceit**.

Choose the best spelling word to complete each sentence. Use each word once.

1. I can't _____ you sneaked into that old house!
2. When she discovered his _____, she knew that he had lied to her.
3. Let's go rent a funny _____ to watch this afternoon.
4. What kind of _____ will you make for dessert?
5. The farmer planted wheat in his _____.
6. The company's _____ wanted to change the selling price.
7. Please help me paint the _____.
8. If a baby bird falls out of its nest, it might _____.
9. Would you like to eat the last _____ of cake?
10. Riding that huge roller coaster was really a thrilling _____!
11. Don't forget to _____ it tightly or it may blow away.
12. Here's your _____ for the purchase of the clothes.
13. She enjoyed reading the books in the Harry Potter _____.
14. The dog went in front of the fireplace to _____ down.
15. When do you think I will _____ the package?

Vowel Pair: "ie" (cont.)

Word Scramble

Unscramble the spelling words. Put each circled letter on the line that matches its number. You will form the answer to the riddle.

1. cieavhe   a   c   h   i   e   v   e
    (1)

2. ceveeir   ___ ___ ___ ___ ___ ___ ___
    (2)

3. cifeh   ___ ___ ___ ___ ___
    (3)

4. eid   ___ ___ ___
    (4)

5. cpreite   ___ ___ ___ ___ ___ ___ ___
    (5)

6. iel   ___ ___ ___
    (6)

7. lfide   ___ ___ ___ ___ ___
    (7)

8. clienig   ___ ___ ___ ___ ___ ___ ___
    (8)

9. tdeiec   ___ ___ ___ ___ ___ ___
    (9)

10. sriees   ___ ___ ___ ___ ___ ___
    (10)

11. peeci   ___ ___ ___ ___ ___
    (11)

12. eit   ___ ___ ___
    (12)

13. voime   ___ ___ ___ ___ ___
    (13)

14. iep   ___ ___ ___
    (14)

15. vleiebe   ___ ___ ___ ___ ___ ___ ___
    (15)

16. eperixenec   ___ ___ ___ ___ ___ ___ ___ ___ ___ ___
    (16)

If a monkey lost its tail, where could it get a new one?

___ ___   ___ ___ ___   ___ ___ ___ a ___ ___   ___ ___ ___ ___ ___
4 8   5 3 11   16 15 9 1 7 6   10 12 13 2 14

Assessment 1

Fill in the circle of the word that is spelled correctly and best completes the sentence.

1. **I hope that _____ coming to my party.**
   - (a) their
   - (b) there
   - (c) they're

2. **The skirt was too _____ for me.**
   - (a) tight
   - (b) tite
   - (c) tiet

3. **Sometime _____ the day, the shed's door cracked.**
   - (a) during
   - (b) dering
   - (c) daring

4. **She's won the blue ribbon _____ in a row!**
   - (a) twisw
   - (b) twice
   - (c) twies

5. **He _____ his name on the check.**
   - (a) wrote
   - (b) rote
   - (c) wroat

6. **Please be _____ going up the ladder.**
   - (a) carfu
   - (b) careful
   - (c) carefull

7. **They ate _____ for breakfast.**
   - (a) serial
   - (b) cerel
   - (c) cereal

8. **I would love to eat a ripe _____.**
   - (a) bannana
   - (b) banana
   - (c) bananna

9. **We _____ all of the addition facts.**
   - (a) know
   - (b) now
   - (c) no

10. **We still need to _____ the subtraction facts.**
    - (a) reviwe
    - (b) review
    - (c) revew

11. **A big _____ had gathered to hear the mayor speak.**
    - (a) croud
    - (b) croude
    - (c) crowd

12. **After three _____, Sam went home.**
    - (a) ours
    - (b) howrs
    - (c) hours

13. **Once you _____ the color, we will make the frame.**
    - (a) choose
    - (b) choice
    - (c) chose

14. **The _____ of the fire is uncertain.**
    - (a) caws
    - (b) caus
    - (c) cause

15. **He's out chopping logs for the _____ stove.**
    - (a) wood
    - (b) would
    - (c) wud

16. **I'm sure that he _____ no harm when he said that to you.**
    - (a) meaned
    - (b) mean
    - (c) meant

17. **Never _____ your teacher.**
    - (a) disoby
    - (b) disobey
    - (c) disoeby

18. **Let's buy a _____ to watch later.**
    - (a) video
    - (b) vidio
    - (c) vidieo

19. **Who gets to eat that last _____ of cherry pie?**
    - (a) peace
    - (b) piece
    - (c) peice

20. **You have your _____ of sizes.**
    - (a) choise
    - (b) chose
    - (c) choice

Assessment 2

Darken the circle of the one word that is spelled correctly in each row.

1. (a) could of   (b) culd've   (c) could've

2. (a) night   (b) nite   (c) niht

3. (a) bilding   (b) billding   (c) building

4. (a) physcal   (b) physical   (c) physicle

5. (a) knowledge   (b) knoleje   (c) knoledge

6. (a) gard   (b) guard   (c) gurad

7. (a) jeneral   (b) genral   (c) general

8. (a) camera   (b) camra   (c) camira

9. (a) follow   (b) folow   (c) flolow

10. (a) threw   (b) thru   (c) throogh

11. (a) towl   (b) towle   (c) towel

12. (a) mounten   (b) mountain   (c) mountin

13. (a) balloon   (b) baloon   (c) ballon

14. (a) anoy   (b) annoy   (c) ennoy

15. (a) dawter   (b) dauter   (c) daughter

16. (a) fut   (b) foote   (c) foot

17. (a) wear   (b) whare   (c) whear

18. (a) valey   (b) valley   (c) vallee

19. (a) pioneer   (b) pioner   (c) piuneer

20. (a) receipt   (b) reciet   (c) receit

Answer Key

Page 4

Are
you're
we're
they're

Have
could've
would've

Will
I'll
you'll
we'll

Not
can't
wasn't
isn't
won't
don't
didn't
doesn't

Page 5

Possible answers:
16. hadn't, hasn't, haven't, wouldn't, couldn't, shouldn't
17. they'll, she'll, he'll, it'll
18. we've, they've, you've, should've

Page 6

1. frighten
2. sigh
3. highway
4. might
5. slightly
6. fight
7. night
8. bright
9. tight
10. knight
11. flight
12. right
13. light
14. high
15. sight

Page 7

Answers will vary with dictionary used.

Page 8

1. OK
2. nothing
3. OK
4. during
5. everything
6. OK
7. OK
8. OK
9. anything
10. morning
11. OK
12. OK

13. building
14. being
15. OK

Page 10

1. twirl
2. graph
3. twist
4. twice
5. physical
6. paragraph
7. twelve
8. elephant
9. phone
10. alphabet
11. twilight
12. twig
13. twin
14. tweezers
15. photo

Page 11

1. twin
2. phone
3. elephant
4. twirl
5. graph
6. twice
7. twig
8. photo
9. twist
10. twelve
11. physical
12. tweezers
13. paragraph
14. twilight
15. alphabet
Riddle answer: It makes sense (cents) to put us together.

Page 12

1. known
2. wreath
3. knife
4. wrap
5. knowledge
6. writer
7. knuckles
8. wreck
9. knit
10. knock
11. wrong
12. wriggle
13. knot
14. wrote
15. wrinkle

Page 13

1. wrap; 9727
2. wreck; 97325
3. wrong; 97664

4. wrote; 97683
5. writer; 974837
6. wreath; 973284
7. wriggle; 9744453
8. wrinkle; 9746553
9. knit; 5648
10. knot; 5668
11. knife; 56433
12. knock; 56625
13. knuckles; 56825537
14. known; 56696
15. knowledge; 566953343

Page 14

1. carry; 2; careful
2. careful; 1; carry
3. could; 5; color
4. come; 4; come
5. color; 3; could
6. cute; 7; curve
7. curve; 6; cute
8. gave; 10; garden
9. garden; 8; gather
10. gather; 9; gave
11. guard; 14; going
12. guess; 15; gone
13. going; 11; government
14. gone; 12; guard
15. government; 13; guess

Page 15

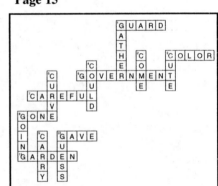

Page 16

1. OK
2. OK
3. OK
4. cider
5. OK
6. OK
7. OK
8. cereal
9. OK
10. celebrate
11. OK
12. OK
13. generous
14. gentle
15. circus

Answer Key (cont.)

Page 17
Hard C
carry
come
careful
could
color
curve
cute

Hard G
government
guess
gone
going
gave
guard
gather
garden

Soft C
certain
cereal
circus
cents
circle
center
celebrate
cider
citizen

Soft G
germ
general
gigantic
gentle
giant
generous

Page 18
1. lava
2. America
3. banana
4. idea
5. extra
6. area
7. pizza
8. Asia
9. comma
10. Antarctica
11. Africa
12. camera
13. china
14. Australia
15. Canada

Page 19
consonants
pizza
comma
extra
china
Antarctica

intersecting circles
banana   Canada
camera   Africa
lava
vowels
idea   Asia
area   Australia
America

Page 20
1. row; rowed; rows
2. grow; no; grows
3. low; no; no
4. blow; no; blows
5. flow; flowed; flows
6. slow; slowed; slows
7. show; showed; shows
8. snow; snowed; snows
9. know; no; knows
10. below; no; no
11. window; no; windows
12. narrow; narrowed; narrows
13. shadow; shadowed; shadows
14. follow; followed; follows
15. owner; no; owners

Page 21
1. slow   9. grow
2. flow   10. follow
3. know   11. shadow
4. snow   12. row
5. window   13. show
6. below   14. owner
7. low   15. narrow
8. blow

Riddle answer: Nothing! He was too shocked.

Page 22
1. grew   9. stew
2. preview   10. knew
3. chew   11. drew
4. flew   12. crew
5. new   13. dew
6. view   14. blew
7. few   15. review
8. threw

Page 23
Answers will vary with dictionary used.

Page 24
1. now & how
2. crowd & loud
3. towel & vowel
4. power & shower
5. down & town
6. flowers & towers
7. cows & plows
8. brown & crown
9. allow
10. however

Page 25
gray
below   shadow
snow   window
owner   known
brown
town   vowel
allow   power
towel   however
shower   crowd
flower

Page 27

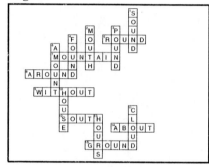

Page 28
1. too; 14; afternoon
2. food; 5; balloon
3. school; 10; choose
4. soon; 13; cool
5. room; 8; food
6. moon; 6; moon
7. root; 9; pool
8. cool; 4; room
9. tool; 15; root
10. pool; 7; school
11. choose; 3; shoot
12. smooth; 12; smooth
13. shoot; 11; soon
14. balloon; 2; too
15. afternoon; 1; tool

Page 29
consonants
school   balloon
smooth   afternoon
shoot
intersecting circles
choose   root
food   cool
soon   tool
room   pool
moon
vowels
too

Page 30
1. join   6. toys   11. avoid
2. employee   7. point   12. noise
3. oil   8. coin   13. destroy
4. loyal   9. annoy   14. enjoy
5. soil   10. choice   15. voice

Answer Key (cont.)

Page 32

1. OK	9. flaw
2. daughter	10. OK
3. OK	11. claws
4. OK	12. automobile
5. cause	13. OK
6. OK	14. caught
7. OK	15. OK
8. OK	

Page 33

1. saw; 729
2. draw; 3729
3. paw; 729
4. jaw; 529
5. raw; 729
6. law; 529
7. claws; 25297
8. flaw; 3529
9. straw; 78729
10. drawing; 3729464
11. cause; 22873
12. caught; 228448
13. daughter; 32844837
14. autumn; 288866
15. automobile; 2886662453
16. saw, paw, raw

Page 34

1. hook	9. good
2. wool	10. brook
3. look	11. wood
4. stood	12. shook
5. foot	13. cook
6. crook	14. nook
7. book	15. hood
8. took	

Page 35

"oo" as in "cool"

The Magic Tool
Full Moon
Come Home Soon
Choose a Game
Smooth as Glass
Shoot the Stars
Hot Air Balloons
The Deep Pool
A Tangled Root
The Dark Room
Play it Cool
Me Too!
Yummy Food
One Scary Afternoon
My Haunted School

"oo" as in "book"

Look Out!
The Wool Cloak
The Attic Nook
Good Times
He Took the Call
The Ugly Hook
The Blue Hood
How to Cook
Hard as Wood
A Silly Book
The Quiet Brook
Monster's Foot
The Secret Crook
It Stood on the Hill
The Day the World Shook

Page 36

1. bread; tread; yes
2. instead; steady; yes
3. ahead; head; yes
4. already; ready; yes
5. heavy; heave; no
6. meant; mean; no
7. death; wreath; no
8. breath; breathe; no
9. weather; feather; yes
10. ocean; clean; no
11. measure; pleasure; yes

Page 37

long "e" loaf

scream	speak
seats	bead
reading	repeat
treat	leaf
steal	

short "e" loaf

already	measure
heavy	ahead
ocean	meant
weather	instead
bread	death
breath	

long "a" loaf

bear	great
wear	break

Page 39

Answers will vary based on dictionary used.

Page 40

1. stereo
2. patio
3. violet
4. Iowa
5. rodeo
6. priority
7. radio
8. trio
9. violin
10. pioneer
11. video
12. prior
13. violent
14. studio
15. ratio

Page 41

Page 42

1. believe	9. piece
2. deceit	10. experience
3. movie	11. tie
4. pie	12. receipt
5. field	13. series
6. chief	14. lie
7. ceiling	15. receive
8. die	

Page 43

1. achieve	9. deceit
2. receive	10. series
3. chief	11. piece
4. die	12. tie
5. receipt	13. movie
6. lie	14. pie
7. field	15. believe
8. ceiling	16. experience

Riddle: In the retail store

Page 44

1. c	11. c
2. a	12. c
3. a	13. a
4. b	14. c
5. a	15. a
6. b	16. c
7. c	17. b
8. b	18. a
9. a	19. b
10. b	20. c

Page 45

1. c	11. c
2. a	12. b
3. c	13. a
4. b	14. b
5. a	15. c
6. b	16. c
7. c	17. a
8. a	18. b
9. a	19. a
10. a	20. a